THE YANTRAS

SRI GARIB DASS ORIENTAL SERIES NO 48

The Yantras

Text with 32 Plates

Prof. S. K. RAMACHANDRA RAO

SRI SATGURU PUBLICATIONS
DELHI—INDIA

Published by :
SRI SATGURU PUBLICATIONS
a division of
INDIAN BOOKS CENTRE,
40/5, Shakti Nagar,
Delhi—110007
INDIA

First Edition—Delhi—1988

I.S.B.N.--81-7030-118-1

Printed at :
Arun Composing Agency
D-102, New Sealampur,
Delhi-110053

CONTENTS

PART II

LIST OF FIGURES

(*Page number and
Paragraph to
which it is related*)

I

INTRODUCTION

The use of mystical designs and magical diagrams, known as "yantras", is of great antiquity, not only in India but in all countries. Among the early archaeological finds are included specimens of such designs and diagrams, which were neither strictly utilitarian nor solely decorative in function. Even before religion became organized and institutionalized in the primitive society, visual representations of magical intentions and ideas were employed, along with charms and spells. They were meant to compel events in an occult manner, events individual in significance as well as collective in import. Intentions included warding off evil, overcoming danger, compelling rain, driving away pestilence, blocking hailstorm, increasing fertility of the soil, ensuring success in hunting or in expedition, restoring health, prolonging life, recovering lost property, defeating the enemy, confounding the opponent, and securing objects of love.

Reason which helped the development of science and technology also brought into being magic and religion. It would be anthropologically unsound to describe scientific thinking as rational and religious thinking as irrational. The crudest of magical procedures were also based on the reasoning faculty. It was human reason that generated the ideas of God, of the spirit, and of the relation that one bore to the other as well as the ideas of matter and energy, and the measurements thereof. Even as technology is based on the desire to control the physical world within and around us, magic is based on the desire to control the spiritual world within and around us.

It is unfortunate that the word 'magic' has acquired a connotation which few modern minds would relish. It is equally unfortunate that all that goes under the banner of science and technology passes as unquestionably and eminently worthwhile. It is owing to the western connotation of the word 'magic' that what has no 'rational' explanation is dubbed as irrational. It is made to appear that magic is sustained on solid superstitions and illusions, while science rests on solid facts which are demonstrable and incontrovertible. However, the student of the history of science is very well aware that science rests not on facts but on assumptions, and that these assumptions with their implications and applications are by no means immutably fixed or altogether incontrovertible.

The word 'magic' originally meant the wisdom of the Eastern mystics ('magus' or 'magi', denoting members of the Persian priestly class). The word is probably derived from the Sanskrit 'magha' which means not only a class of people (Cf. the lexicon *Medinī*), but 'great wealth' (Cf. *Ṛgveda*, 7, 2', 7 'endowed by the chief of the gods Indra, who possesses it in plenty, hence called Maghavān) and 'best medicine' (in the feminine form of the word Cf. the lexicon *Dhāraṇī*). The word 'magha' is cognate with "mahat" (from *maghash*), which means undifferentiated consciousness (*buddhi*, as distinguished from individualized consciousness or ego, *ahamkāra*, and objective consciousness or *manas*). Magic is thus actually an aspect of knowledge which concerns consciousness ; it seeks to understand the dynamics of consciousness, to train consciousness and to apply it to secure personal and collective welfare.

It is true that the word magic has came to signify the art of controlling external objects or compelling events, and of projecting objects and events which lack solid reality. And magic is usually related in our minds with witchcraft, sorcery, charlatanry, abracadabra, illusions, hoax and make-beliefs. Thus, magic appears as an enemy of science and as an outrage on decency. The blame is not altogether unfounded either. Centuries of magical practices and generations of magicians have contributed enormously to justify this denunciation. It cannot be denied that magical ideas and practices have thriven mainly on the gullibility and ignorance of the people, inviting exploitation by cheats and rogues.

But to condemn magic on this score would be like denouncing science and technology, pointing at the explosives, pollutants, poisons and other hazards that they have brought into being. Magic for illicit and unscrupulous gain is not the essential or original aspect of magic. There is no denying that magic, being basically a practical discipline, is an art and has autilitarian overtone. Religion is the theoretical side, the counterpart of science, and magic is one of its applications, even as technology is an application of science. Religion has its foundation in reason, and is based on experience and intuition. The reason that it upholds may be of a kind different than what science insists on, but it is nevertheless valid human reason which has stood mankind in good stead for countless generations that have gone by, and which is likely to hold away over humanity for countless generations to come. Magic, as an applicative art, works within the framework thus set by religion, and formulates its own special variety of reason to supplement what religion works by.

Religion seeks to 'relate' (as the etymological significance of the word demands) individual consciousness to the undifferentiated consciousness. This it seeks to achieve in a variety of ways, depending on the culture of the people, geography of the place, and the history of the community. Thus there are variant idioms characteristic of religion, each of them providing the outfit of a distinct subculture. Magic as the practical outcome of religion seeks to involve the undifferentiated consciousness within the field of individual consciousness. If religion is interested in raising the individual to a higher plane (called spiritual in a general sense), magic is interested in bringing down the denizens of this higher plane to the normal work-a-day world. Religion expects to smooth out the odd angularities of the human being, and to break down the sharp boundaries that delimit the outlook of the lay folk, and thus to 'undifferentiate' the individual. Magic, on the other hand, expects to 'differentiate' the amorphous and nebulous spiritual world, thus individualizing the undifferentiated. Religion is a move towards generalization and the universal, while magic moves in the direction of specification and the individual. Religion appears more rational than magic, inasmuch as it proceeds from the known world of the individual, a world which is concrete (in the sense of being amenable to sense-perception), verifiable, familiar, and possessing of what may be called public reality. Magic, however, proceeds from an abstract world, the reality of which is rather assumed than perceived, the reality which may properly be described as private. Religion starts with normal reason and works its way upwards beyond common reason, whereas magic starts with what is beyond common reason, and comes down eventually to a world of common reason. Thus, magic when viewed from the standpoint of common reason has a ring of the irrational. This is also the reason why fooling, deceit, trickery and exploitation abound in the field of magic. It is indeed a world of 'make-believe', as far as lay reason can make anything out of it.

But magic, in its original and essential sense, has its own rationale, its own reason, its own logic, its own idiom. It rejects the ultimacy of the objects of sense-perception, and the exclusive reality of the contents and methods of the world of our common experience. It posits a 'world' which is invisible but real, abstract but effective, subtle but manageable ; and argues that the world which is visible, concrete and gross is but small aspect of this 'world'. Are there not organs and details in our body which are not only invisible to us but of which we are altogether unaware ? And then science discovers extremely subtle ingredients of the human constitution that do not belong to the world in which we live, move and function. Religion points to the world within the individual, which we are normally not aware of, the inner world of consciousness. And magic points to the world within the 'world', of which again we are not normally aware, as it were the outer world of consciousness. When we speak of the individual in the world, we prefer to ignore the inner world of the individual's consciousness as well as the world of consciousness outside the individual. We tend to look upon the individual as a detail of the world, partaking of its character of concrete reality. The abstract world within the concrete individual and the abstract individuals within the concrete world are alike lost sight of.

Magic is in reality an attempt to map this abstract world and delineate the abstract individuals The tāntrik ideology of the human being as constituted by several 'chakras' (*mūlādhāra, svādhiṣṭhāna, maṇipūra* etc.) is an illustration of this endeavour. It is unprofitable to seek to identify the presence of these 'chakras' within the anatomical and physiological constitution of man, or to work out correspondances between the text-specific 'chakras' and the observable organs and functions of the body. The 'chakras' are in reality centres of an abstract world within the individual, altogether inaccessible to our normal perception and even common reason. The well-known 'Śrī-chakra' is likewise a map of the abstract cosmos that corresponds both with the abstract world within the individual and with the abstract individuals within the concrete world.

This world of magic is indeed a network of energies, forces and vectors. It is more dynamic than the world we are normally acquainted with. The constructs of space and time are not the same in the two worlds ; the logic of events too is different. The language that man has developed during his career on this planet is thoroughly inadequate to describe the abstract world of magic. The linguistic habits that man has acquired in order to transact effectively in this concrete world are found to be irrelevant, if he should convey his innermost experiences and his intuitive apprehension of the inner world of spirit. But that is the only tool that man is acquainted with, in order to communicate with his fellow-beings.

In accordance with the needs of the concrete individual living in a matter-of-fact world, language also becomes necessarily concrete and practical. Those who are familiar with the world of magic and would desire to communicate with others would perforce have to use this same language, but make some alterations and evolve some rules of the game. The *mantra*, for instance, apparently makes use of the language that we all use, but the intentions contained in it are more suggestive than explicit, more esoteric than actual, more private than public. The *mantra* is rather in the nature of a caricature.

In the Tāntrik framework, the *mantra* has its own grammar, its own semantics, its own mnemomic ideology. The tantra looks upon the Sanskrit alphabet as the network of abstract and primordial sound-units (*varṇa*), each sound-unit (or letter) being a specific energy. The abstract forces that work within the individual and in the world outside are amenable to influences from these sound-units. The energetics of the individual are thus sought to be augmented, enhanced, corrected and rendered effective by the employment of the *mantra*. Not any *mantra* would work for any individual, of course ; the sound-units need to be matched with the energy dynamics specific to each individual. The selection of a *mantra* for the individual is made considering his constitution, physical as well as mental, the cultural milieu, his inclinations, and needs.

Another medium of magic (viz. the Tantra) is the *yantra*, or visual representation of the energies, forces and vectors that operate within the individual at the abstract level and are present as the invisible world within the world that we know of. The *yantra* is naturally very closely related to the undifferentiated consciousness that comprehends both the individual and the physical world around him. The *mantra* utilizes the verbal symbols while the *yantra* makes use of graphic designs. Even as the entire linguistic behaviour of man is reduced to the essential and undying sound-units (*bīja-aksharas*) in the *mantra*, the whole of the visible world available to man is reduced to the essential and universal form-units (such as the point, the circle, the triangle, the square) in the *yantra*.

fig. 1, 2 and 3

Magical spells and mystical diagrams in some form or other have always been parts of human heritage. In India, the seals recovered from the sites of the so-called Indus Valley civilization (dating back to more than three thousand years before Christ), leave no doubt that the cult of the mystical diagrams was prevalent among those people. There are also references in the Vedic lore, especially in the *Atharva* collection, to the use of charms, spells and mystic diagrams. Magic in these texts were coersive as well as curative ; it was employed for securing welfare as well as for undoing evil. Numerous herbs were used along with spells. The curious connection of medicine with magic that we find here is not an isolated phenomenon ; it was prevalent in all cultures.

In the *Atharva* collection can be found the twofold division of magic ; benevolent (*atharva*) and malefic (*āṅgiras*). The former division included the rites that were meant to secure health, happiness, welfare (*Śāntika, paushṭika*, etc) of the individual as well as the community, while the latter division was illustrated by sorcery and witchcraft (*abhichāra, ghora, māraṇa, yātu, kṛtya*, etc). However. it was the former division that was regarded as significant and worthwhile. The latter division was indicated because according to the Ātharvaṇic ideology, the subtle and invisible world was peopled by malevolent spirits, which cause disease and distress, discomfort and embarassment. Many of them are named : Chaṇḍā, Arāyi, Koka, Durnāma, Arjunī, Grāhi, Nirṛti, Sadāhva, Ugrajihvā, Malimlucha, Pramāli, Kakūrabha and so on. There are passages indicating how they can be propitiated, and thereby softened and turned favourable.

The benevolent magic, envisaged in *Atharva-veda*, is essentially folk in character. Situations in which it is indicated include self-defence, protection of house and property, health of oneself and cattle success in enterprise, housewarming, consecration of newly constructed tank etc , safety of household, safe delivery, recovery of lost property, obtainment of knowledge, improvement of memory, enhancing physical charm, exorcism, gaining wealth. commanding good luck, winning affection, prevention of natural catastrophe and avoidance of accidents. Besides spells, various charms from herbs (*apāmārga, rohiṇī, dūrva, audumbara, palāsa* etc.) and animal products (antelope's horn, tiger's paw, wild boar's tooth etc.) and metals (copper, iron, gold etc.) were prepared and employed. Designs and diagrams drawn on the ground or wall, or on leather or metal were also used for magical benefits.

Many of these customs have survived till our own day, and are prevalent among the people, especially of the rural parts. They have been incorporated in popular Hinduism, and are extensively used, although the sophisticated Indian thought shuns them. The benevolent magic (*śānti*, pacification of evil spirits so that the individual is happy ; *paushṭika*, nourishment of the individual viz. fulfilment of normal needs ; *bheshaja*, cure of diseases and restoration of health) has become very much the part of lay religion. Spells and charms are extensively employed to secure health, wealth and happiness, along with the worship of divinities and the performance of sacrifices and other rituals according to Vedic prescriptions.

The malefic magic (sorcery, witchcraft, black magic, e.g. *vaśīkaraṇa*, attracting the affection of people by coercion ; *stambhana*, arresting the movement or speech of opponents ; *vidveshana*, causing enmity and ill-will among friends ; *ucchāṭana*, throwing out enemies by occult influence, *māraṇa*, causing death) is naturally frowned upon by the cultured folk (*śishta*) and is not resorted to by common folk. It is confined to small and secretive pockets in the countryside, and the practitioners of this art are invariably regarded as wicked ; they are objects of fear and revulsion, and are treated almost as outcastes.

They claim, of course falsely, to exercise influence over spirits of all sorts (mostly imps and goblins, demons of disease and disaster, bearing frightful names and having hideous forms), and to be able to pressurize them favourably or otherwise on behalf of their clients. The interesting detail in this context is the large and variegated repertoir of spells, charms, designs and diagrams that the practitioners of this dark and dangerous art possess. While many of these spells are little more than jibberish and most drawings plainly nonsensical, it must be conceded that some of them are highly significant as verbal or visual representations of intense and violent emotions

II

What are Yantras ?

The expression 'yantra' is derived from the root "yam" (*Uṇādi* 4,133) or alternatively from the form 'yantrati' (or 'yantrayati') (*Dhātu-pātha, 32,3*), the meaning in both cases being "to restrain", "to compel", "to bend". The early context in which the word was used relates to mechanical contrivances. The 'yantra' in this context is an engine, a machine, an appliance. As instances may be cited 'gṛha-yantra' (pole in front of the house or on top of the house to fasten festoons and flags), 'kūpa-yantra', (contrivance for drawing water from the well), 'taila-yantra' (apparatus for extracting oil), 'yantropala' (mill-stone), 'yantra-gṛha' (oil-mill), 'dāru-yantra' (a wooden appliance for rotating) and 'yantra-putrikā' (puppet or doll which is moved by strings). There is a reference in the *Bhagavad gītā* to the puppets mounted on a revolving apparatus ('yantrārūḍhāni', 18, 61). Probably this refers to a toy or a 'merry-go-round'. Many 'yantras' are mentioned in ancient and medieval works on astronomy, architecture, alchemy and allied disciplines.

The word is also applied to surgical instruments, especially the blunt ones (as distinguished from the cutting instruments, which were called 'śastras'). *Suśruta-saṁhitā*, the well-known surgical treatise of ancient India, mentions several 'yantras' such as 'saṁdaṁśa-yantra' (gripping instruments), 'tala-yantra' (discs with handle), 'nāḍī-yantra' (tubular appliances) and 'śalākya-yantra' (thin probes). There are also 'accessory appliances' known as 'upa-yantras'.

It was not till a late date that the expression 'yantra' came be employed to suggest mystic designs and magical diagrams. This employment was justified by the connotation of the word 'yantra-ṇam' ('yantra' with lyuṭ suffix) as 'protection' 'guarding', 'restraining' or 'binding', (rakashaṇam, bandhanam, niyamanam), which is an extension of the etymological meaning 'conserving' or 'limiting' ('yantṛ saṁkochane'). We find that *Suśruta saṁhitā* also employs the word in this sense.

The employment of such designs as instrumental to protection was an ancient practice, and specimens of them have been recovered from the dim past in all countries, especially in the Eastern countries. Drawings, ritualistically prepared by qualified priests and shamans, were believed to possess unusual, uncanny and extraordinary power ; it was also believed that the intentions and expectations of the individual using them would be fulfilled easily, almost without effort, and surely, without an exception. Being a ritualistic detail, great care was attached not only to the preparation of these protective devices but to the mode of their employment also. There were different designs for different protective purposes : protection of the person, protection of the household, protection of the property, protection of the cattle, protection of the people, protection of the buildings and so on. There were community designs, inscribed on rocky surfaces owned collectively, and attended to by the whole community. There were also personal and private designs drawn on paper (*rekhā-yantra*) inscribed on metals, either placed in the household and worshipped by the members of the family (*pūjā-yantra*) or worn by a person on his body as an amulet or talisman (*dhāraṇa-yantra*).

The protective power that is supposed to be possessed by a yantra lies in the shape of the design. The shape, consisting of one or more of geometric forms interwoven to constitute a whole pattern, is believed to represent the spirit or spirits that one seeks to communicate with, in order to derive strength and succour.

The *yantra* is in the nature of a field for the spirits to dwell and to function. Every *yantra* is a self sufficient, self-contained, complete and closed realm, well-guarded against out ide interfere-nces, as indicated by the sharp boundary lines which invariably surround the principal design of the *yantra*. The boundary lines are meant not only to preserve the nature of this magical power contained in the main design (usually the central portion) but to prevent the diffusion of this power. The other geometrical patterns involved in the *yantra* serve to augment the magical power, to enhance the quality, and to facilitate the movement of energies in the desired direction.

The forms involving points, lines, triangles and squares repre-sent energies in various modes. The point (*bindu*) is the focal aspect of energy. It is the intense concentration of energy, which functions like a store-house from which energy is derived by the other forms. It is described as the 'home' of the spirit, whose estate is the space comprehended by the *yantra*. When the spirit is also symbolized by a seed-syllable (*bīja-akshara*), this imper-ishable seed-syllable is inscribed on the point. The point is surrounded by successive enclosures, viz, a traingle, two traingles intersecting, a circle, and so on. These forms indicate outward manifestation of the spirit so as to exert its influence in the desired manner. A line denotes movement of the spirit, or line of energy ; a triangle represents a concerted pattern of three fold energy lines. The lines of the triangle are described as the aspects or attendants of the Spirit.

The intersections of simple forms (lines, triangle, squares etc.) are regarded as more powerful, as they involve dynamic interaction of energy-lines. The spaces formed by these intersections are described as especial fields of operation of the influence, emanating from the Spirit (whose home is the central point or *bindu*). Seed-syllables, associated with the Spirit, are therefore inscribed in them. Sometimes an entire formula is accommodated within these spaces. The power possessed by the *yantra* is sought to be stepped up by the inscription of appropriate *mantra* in it, for the *yantra* and the *mantra* are two complementary aspects of the Spirit, and the two together can be more effective than each alone.

When the *yantra* is prepared for the protection of a particular person, the name of that person is written in the focal section of the *yantra*, very close to the 'home' of the spirit which is invoked as the protector. In the specimen *yantras* given in manuals, the location for this purpose is indicated by the words 'sādhya-nāma' (or the name of the possible recipient of the Spirit's protective power), or by the expression ('Deva-datta' signifying any name that is appropriate, as in the English expression. Tom, Dick or Harry'). The underlying idea is that the name of a person has a magical property and can officiate for the individual in his entirety. The first letter of a name is a significant detail, and is taken into consideration for the selection of a *mantra* suitable for that person.

The *yantras* are mainly graphic representations involving geometrical designs. But sometimes, figures of arrow-heads, spears, tridents, swords, maces and other weapons are also included to represent the vectors of the energies that operate within the field. It is usual to transform a square as an assembly of four tridents placed so as to enclose the field of energy dynamics. The trident is a defensive weapon, weilded by the master of Spirits, viz Śiva. It symbolises that protection is assured. It is also usual to transform a circle as an open lotus, petals of each of which represents an enclosure for energy-dynamics. The lotus is a symbol of purity as well as multi-dimensionality; it also signifies the creative process. The lotus in the yantra, thus represents freedom from interference from the outside (purity), manifold expression of the Spirit, and the emanation of the influence, reaching out.

The possible *yantras* are indeed innumerable. The combinations of the primary geometrical forms (triangles, circles and four-sided figures) can be myriad, and the association of *mantras* with the designs render the number of these combinations really huge. There is a Sanskrit text, comparatively recent, which enumerates as many as 10,000 *yantras* ! The name of this text is *Yantroddhāra-sarvasva,* and the author (anonymous) claims that he obtained all these *yantras* from *Atharva-veda,* not, however, explaining how. The largest well-known collection, however, is to be found as the supplementary section to *Saundarya-laharī,* ascribed to the great Śaṁkara : it contains 103 *yantras* with details concerning their use known as 'prayoga'. Another text *Yantra-chintāmaṇi* contains about eighty *'yantras'* ; *Mantra-mahodadhi* describes about seventy, *Prapañcha-sāra-saṁgraha* about sixty, *Prayoga-kaumudī* about fifty, *Mantra-yantra-mahārṇava* about the same number. Other texts like *Kāma-ratna, Maṇi-mantra-kosha, Devatā-pūjana-vidhi, Yantra-prakāśa, Yantra-pratishthā* and *Yantra-pūjana-prakāra* also contain numerous illustrations of *yantras.*

The yantras are generally classified into two types : (1) devices for worship (*pūjana-yantras*), and (2) devices for protection (*rakshā-yantras*). The former are 'deity-specific' (*devatā nirdishṭa*), each classical divinity having a *yantra* of its own. Thus, we not only have the Devī-yantras, Vishṇu-yantras and Śiva-yantras, but there are *yantras* for the several forms which these main divinities assume : e.g. Tripurā-yantra, Durgā-yantra, Śūlinī-yantra, Narasiṁha-yantra, Krishṇa-yantra, Dakshiṇāmūrti-yantra, Kālī-yantra, Chāmuṇḍā-yantra, Cchinna-mastā-yantra, Pratyaṅgirā yantra, Mṛtyuñjaya-yantra. Besides these, there are *yantras* for minor or attendant deities (like Hanumān, Garuḍa, Vīrabhadra, Ganeśa, Śāstā, Bhairava, Khaḍga, Yoginī etc.). The spirits of regional importance are also represented in *yantras* (e.g. Yallamma, Kāṭerī, Kuṭṭi-chāttan, Bhagavatī, Kollūramma). All these *yantras* are meant for continued worship and have no specific need motivating their use,

The latter group of *yantras* are more general in character, and are meant to provide protection from a variety of ills and dangers. There are protective and curative *yantras* included in this group. A large number of these *yantras* are merely magical in intent, and are meant to be used for specific purposes, for a specified length of time. Situations which indicate their use include illnesses of various kinds, diseases of the cattle, fear of thieves and robbers, anxiety due to possible attack by enemies, fear of death, troubles concerning delivery, pests on the farm, ill-will from the near ones, alienated affection, bad dreams and nightmares, uncertain outcome of a new enterprise, making progress in studies and acquiring wealth. The value of a *yantra* in this group is limited to the purpose for which it is prepared. A few *yantras*, however, are omnibus in nature, and claim to secure alround welfare.

It is found feasible to combine the two types of *yantras* mentioned above. Some deities are celebrated for their power to bestow on their devotees specific benefits, e.g. Gaṇesa for success in all undertakings, Hanumān for freedom from threats, fear, illness and anxiety, Narasiṁha for preventing calamities, Svarṇabhairava for acquiring wealth, Śiva for long life, Pratyaṅgirā for counteracting black magic, Durgā for protection against evil, and Khaḍga-rāvaṇa for protection of childern from diseases and for warding off the 'black-eye'.

There is a third type of *yantras*, strictly to be called *maṇḍalas*, which are useful in ceremonial sequences (like consecrating the place of worship, placement of the ritual jar or *kalaśa*, placement of the lamp symbolizing god or goddess, preparing the ground for making food-offerings or *naivedya*), in the initiatory rites (*dīkshā-vidhi*) and as aids in meditations (*dhyāna*). The folk design known as (or *raṅgavali*), which has now turned out to be a purely decorative art, was originally meant as a protective device ; to protect the house from evil influences, to protect the place where an auspicious function is to take place from possible harm, to sanctify the ground on which worship is conducted.

Some texts (like *Krama-dīpaka, Maṇḍala-vidhi* and *Vāstu-vīdyā*) make a distinction between *yantras* and *maṇḍalas*. The latter word signifies a decorative motif ('maṇḍayati bhūshayati'), which also focusses attention o1 the essential details ('maṇḍam lāti').. It is usually circular in shape (hence chandra-maṇḍala, sūrya-maṇḍa'a, tejo-maṇḍala), and signifies the spread of light or lustre, influence or impact uniformly alround. Th: *maṇḍala* is the natural extension of the central point (*bindu*). If the central point is the unmanifest power (*avyakta*), the *maṇḍala* is the manifest counterpart thereof (*vyakta*). The *maṇḍala* has therefore invariably a central point, while a *yantra* may or may not have it. The constituent areas of the *maṇḍala* are grouped around the central point, and have thus a certian symmetry of arrangement, suggesting harmony and balance.

The ideology of the *maṇḍala* allows the aspirant or devotee to symbolically enter into the *maṇḍala* and partake of the power that resides within. The *maṇḍala* in this sense is a world in itself, nay the entire cosmos in miniature. It is rightly called a 'cosmogram'. All the worlds, the legendary divisions of the universe, are accommodated within the maṇḍala, the central point being identified with the Deity in one of its incarnations. Thus, the *maṇḍala* is essentially symbolic in significance. The more elaborate *maṇḍalas* are large in size, sometimes big enough for groups of devotees to sit or move around within their precincts. A *yantra*, contrarily, is always small in size, even when elaborate. The *maṇḍala* being symbolic, has use for colours, each colour signifying a passion or a process, a deity, or a demon. The *yantras*, however, are seldom coloured, and even when coloured, colour symbolism is not a relevant detail ; colour is more or less a decorative detail.

Barring these few particulars, *yantras* and *maṇḍalas* belong to the same category of devices for focussing, channelling, and communicating power. There are many *yantras* which, like *maṇḍalas* represent not only the entire physical universe but human accomplishments also They involve portals (*dvāra*) facing the four cardinal directions (East, South, West and North); and the corners of the square boundary (called earth stretch, ***bhūpura***) signify the four intermediate quarters (South East, South-West, North-East and North-West). They represent also the guardian-angels of these eight directions (*loka-pāla*), with their characteristic weapons (*āyudha*), symbolized by specific seed-syllables (*bīja–aksharas*) : (1) East ruled over by Indra, whose weapon is the thunderbolt (*vajra*, 'vam'); (2) South East ruled over by Agni, whose weapon is the spear known as *śakti* ('śam') : (3) South ruled over by Yama, whose weapon is the mace (*daṇḍa*, 'dam'); (4) South West ruled over by Nirṛti, whose weapon is sword (*khaḍga*, 'kham'); (5) West ruled over by Varuṇa, whose weapon is noose (pāśa, 'pam'); (6) North West ruled over by Vāyu, whose weapon is goad (aṅkuśa 'am'); (7) North ruled over by Chandra, whose weapon is mace (*gadā*, 'gam'); and (8) North East ruled over by Īśāna. whose weapon is trident (*triśūla*, 'trīm').

Often, a lotus with eight petals is made to represent this detail. There is also a schema by means of which the letters of the Sanskrit alphabet (with the nasal symbol, *anusvāra*) are all accommodated in the lotus of eight petals. The sixteen vowels are inscribed outside the lotus, often inbetween the petals (called "kesara-sthāna"), and the thirty-five consonants inside the petals. The group of five consonants beginning with 'ka' is accommodated in the petal to the East; the group of five consonants beginning with 'cha' in the petal to the South East; the group of consonants beginning with 'ṭa' in the petal to the South; the group of five consonants beginning with 'ta' in the petal to the South-West; the group of five consonants beginning with 'pa' in the petal to the West; the four consonants beginning with 'ya' in the petal to the North-West; the four consonants beginning with 'śa' in the petals to the North and the two letters 'ḷa' and 'ksha' in the petal to the North-East Such a representation emphasizes the essential identity of the material universe in space and time with the world of articulated speech in human transaction.

Further, the *mandala* signifies the twin acts of emanation and absorption that are not only fundamental to phenomenal existence but the essential nature of all the modalities of manifested consciousness. As was suggested earlier, the central point (*bindu*) marks the transition from the unmanifest (*avyakta*) to the manifest (*vyakta*) condition. The entire world (of thing, speech and mind) evolves in significant stages from the central point, and finally gets dissolved in it. The central point, in one schema, evolves into a triangle, the triangle into a square, and the square into a circle. Most of the geometric patterns involved in *maṇḍalas* are combinations of the triangle (*trikoṇa*), the square (*chatushkoṇa*) and the circle (*vṛtta*). These are different modes of the manifested central point (*vyakta-bindu*), which is itself an unmanifest *maṇḍala* (*avyakta-maṇḍala*).

It is important to remember that the central point is also the undifferentiated but individualized consciousness (*chitta*). The modalities like the triangle, the square and the circle are so many emanations from this source, and they indicate diffusion of the original power into so many diverse forces. The employment of a *maṇḍala* for purposes of meditation involves gathering up of the forces and focussing consciousness into the central point. Incidental to this is the acquisition of power : the mind that is concentrated is powerful, while the mind that is scattered is weak. Thoughts and feelings that are diffuse characterize the normal man. Meditation is the technique of settling them, focussing them in some system.

Maṇḍala in this sense provides the model for experiencing reality, for re-integration, for self-actualization. It accommodates not only the modalities of the transactional world but even the unconscious processes. The underlying idea is that there is no inherent dichotomy between the external and internal realities, between the physical universe and the psychological world. Things and thoughts are but different modalities of the self-same spirit, whose real nature is undifferentiated consciousness (*chitta-mātra*). This is the significance of the Tāntrik statement that "*saṃsāra* and *moksha* are one". The *maṇḍala* is a graphic representation of this idea.

III

The Three Varieties of Yantra

From what has been said in the previous section, it would have become clear that the *yantra,* being essentially an instrument for some accomplishment, falls into different types, in accordance with the objectives of the accomplishments. In this book, three major types of *yantras* will be considered and illustrated : (1) *yantras* for magical purposes, generally called 'protective yantras' (*rakshā-yantras*) : (2) *yantras* for actualizing divinities (*devatā-yantras*) ; and (3) *yantras* that facilitate meditation (*dhyāna-yantras*). In the first variety, the power infused into the *yantra* by the adept is the most important consideration, and the subject (for whose benefit it is prepared) has only to receive it, keep it, wear it, or honour it in some simple manner. It is a completely em-powered device, drawing upon the standard theories and practices of folk religion. The second variety is meant for worship in stylized ways, and hence also known as 'pūjana-yantras'. The third variety is highly sophisticated, with complicated symbolic significance woven into the fabric of the lines and figures.

Is it obviously the first variety that is most often used by the people, as little exertion is expected of them. And exclusive reliance is made on the supernormal power of the accredited saints and ṭāntrikas who prepare and deliver these *yantras* along with their blissings and spells. These *yantras* are in the nature of charms or talisman, for their influence is occult and immediate, physical and direct. Their potency varies according to the degree of the magical prowess of the tāntrik who prepares them and infuses power into them. It is natural that these *yantras* fulfil their objectives to the measure of faith which the users bring to bear while attending to them.

There are broadly two categories discernible in these magical *yantras* : (a) beneficient ones (*saumya* or *aghora*), and (b) the malevolent ones (*krūra* or *ghora*). The former kind of *yantras* are employed to ward off evil, cure diseases, bring about peace of mind, recover lost property, help growth of children, facilitate trade or agriculture, gain celebrity, win affection of people, success in studies and so on. These are collectively known as "devices for peace and prosperity" (*śāntika-paushṭika*). The latter kind of *yantras* are meant to kill the enemy or harm him in occult fashion, to confound his mind and drive him mad, to uproot him from his habitat, to bring about enmity between two friends, to invoke misfortune on a household, to forcefully prevent functions like speech and mobility and so on. They are collectively known as "vengeful missiles" (*abhichāra*) or "violent acts" (*kṛtyā*).

It is remarkable that the largest number of *yantras* which belong to the first variety ('magical'), and specimens of which are extant, answer to the description of the latter category (viz malevolent). It does not, however, mean that people resort to the *yantras* more often to do harm to others than to do good to themselves. Actually, the employment of the 'beneficient' *yantras* is more universal, more frequent, and more acceptable to the popular imagination. But these *yantras* are usually small in size, familiar in nature, and brief in their career. And they are prepared easily by elders in the family or by priests and ritual officiants ; their preparation requires little of technical skill and less of caution that the malevolent *yantras* invariably entail. The most important factor here is honest goodwill on the part of one who prepares the *yantras*. And, therefore, these *yantras* are generally sought from well-wishers of the person or household. This is how the 'beneficient' *yantras* are lost sight of, despite their popularity.

The 'malevolent' *yantras*, on the other hand, are not generally or readily resorted to by the people. They are required only in conditions of violent hatred, long-standing feuds, bitter strife, quickened passions, and utter despair. People who seek recourse to them are by no means respectable folk. Inclination for these *yantras* is associated with baser values of life : meanness, wickedness, vengeance, avarice, cruelty and disregard for decency. And the tāntriks who specialize in the preparation and use of these *yantras* are also far from respectability : they are more feared and abhorred than respected. This has already been referred to earlier But the matter bears repitition because of the widespread belief in the efficacy of this "black art". Whether these malevolent *yantras* are effective or not, they surely have an unfavourable impact on the practitioners of this art, viz. on those who prepare, prescribe and employ these *yantras*. The evil thoughts are harmful to those who think them ; wicked designs hurt the designers themselves.

One of the favourite themes of 'magical' *yantras* is what is known as 'vaśīkaraṇa' or charming a person one desires. It strictly falls under the malevolent category, because the person desired is compelled (against his or her will) to seek the person using the *yantras*. It is usually the wife of another person or a woman who is indifferent or averse who is thus victimized. There are many *yantras* that are meant to achieve this result. But the scope is not necessarily confined to illicit love or sexual compulsion. To make oneself attractive and desirable in the eyes of all people, especially people in authority, is the more general theme. The recurrent words in the spell associated with such *yantras* are : "Make all people come under my influence (sarva-janam me vaśaṃ ānaya)". A variant theme is making oneself effective, successful and honoured in assemblies, royal courts, debates and shows of skill. In this sense, these *yantras* are more properly to be classed under the 'beneficent' category.

There are other *yantras* which could be classed either under the 'beneficent' or under the 'malevolent' category. An illustration is the *yantra* which seeks to undo the normal effects of unfavourable planetary conjuctions. It is pacificatory (*śāntika*) as well as a missile to drive away the antagonistic forces (*ucchāṭana*). Similarly, the *yantra* to eliminate the diabolical possession (*bhūta-ucchāṭana* or *bhūta-āveśa-nigraha* is both beneficient and malevolent.

In all these magical devices, the mind of the person who needs them is sought to be "programmed" (to use a modern expression), so that the mind has something to focuss its energies on ; the diffuse consciousness is channelized towards greater integration ; anxiety is thus alleviated, and the mind becomes more dynamic. The *yantras*, by their own inner logic and characterestic structures, have something intimate to do with the modes of consciousness that are ridden with fear, anxiety, frustration and aspiration. The occult forces that abound in such *yantras* are said to interact with the energy-dynamics of the person for whom the *yantras* are meant. Thus the usefulness of the *yantras* consists in reorganizing the individual's own field of awareness, rather than making an impact on conditions outside the individual.

They are rightly called "protective devices' (*rakshā-yantras*), for they do prevent the individual's disintegration that would otherwise be the consequence of extreme fear or anxiety, frustration or anguish. The person who prepares the yantras must be capable of exerting this salutary influence on the subjects. It is the subject's faith in such a person's unquestioned occult powers that make the *yantras* effective. Faith is the bridge between the subject's troubled interior and the wholesome and potent psyche of the person who is approached for help. No magic works unless on the sure foundation of faith, and all healing is in effect an act of magic.

The second major type f *yantras* relate to the actualization of specific divinities through worship rituals. There are some divinities that personify magical potency. Hanumān, Vīrabhadra, Khaḍga-Rāvaṇa, Kārtavīrya, Bagalā, Chhinnamastā and Svarṇa-bhairava are instances. Each of these divinities is associated with a particular mode of consciousness. Hanumān, for instance, is invoked in conditions of fear and anxiety. Vīrabhadra is invoked when the subject is confronted with insurmountable difficulties. Khaḍga-Rāvaṇa when invoked is said to cure the ailments of children caused by evil spirits (*bāla-graha*). Kārtavīrya's aid is sought to recover lost property and to banish the fear of thiefs and robbers.

The *yantras* associated with such divinities are actually 'magical' *yantras*, and may rightly be grouped under the variety we have just now considered. The difference between the two varieties consists in the former being essentially devices meant to reorganize the subject's psyche by graphic manipulations alone while the latter variety of *yantras* seek to achieve the same effect by involving a traditionally stylized divinity into the graphic representation. Hence, the latter group of *yantras* are said to be deity-specific (*devatā-yantras*).

The deity-specific *yantras* are different from the magical ones in still another detail : their possessions alone will not be of much good ; to be effective, they entail the performance of certain appropriate worship-rituals. These *yantras* are like icons : they acquire potency only when they are properly attended to. That is to say, the devotee must use this kind of *yantras* only as props for his sustained efforts ; and it is the effort that is, in actuality, significant.

In the deity-specific *yantras*, the deity is often represented by the seed-syllable (*bīja-akshara*) appropriate to the deity, inscribed at the central point (*bindu*). Sometimes the whole *mantra* ascribed to the deity is written within the area of the *yantra*. The attendant-divinities (*parivāra-devatās*) may also be accommodated in different areas of the *yantra*. The *yantra* in such a case is regarded as the realm or kingdom of the deity, various aspects of the *yantra* signifying different emanations of the deity in terms of attendants, associates, functions, modes, instruments, and accomplishments. The *yantra* is looked upon as the entire universe in miniature ; and, therefore, included in the representations are the eight directions, the guardians of the directions, the planets, the elements and the presiding divinities, Simple figures (the point, straight line, cross, triangle, circle) are assigned symbolic significances, and are made to constitute complex figures (square, hexagon, pentagon double cross, star, svastika, lotus etc.), each representing a phenomenal process. The entire *yantra* with all its complex structure is to be viewed as the play-field of the deity who is represented at the central point (*bindu*).

The worship ritual enables the devotee to enter into this field and move in close proximity to the deity. The *mantra* that is specific to the deity is supposed to be powerful enough, if properly communicated and assiduously recited, to transform the phenomenal consciousness of the devotee into deity-conciousnes. An authoritative text says : "The *yantra* has a *mantra* as its soul ; and the deity is the soul of the mantra" (*Kaulāvalī*). The entire *mantra* is condensed (or rather potentized) in the seed-syllable (*bīja-akshara*), which is the verbal form of the deity. By attending to the seed-syllable, the mental form of the deity is actualized. From the seed syllable the *mantra* evolves ; from the *mantra* the *yantra* evolves. All extensions terminate in a point ; and all verbalizations dissolve in a seed-syllable ; and all thoughts end in the deity. There is thus a correspondance between the deity, the central point and the seed-syllable. There is also a correspondance between the *mantra*, the *yantra* and the dimensions of the devotee's consciousness.

The deity-specific *yantras* involve worship ritual; in which the deity is invoked by the appropriate mantra and visualized in the appropriate *yantra*. The anthropomorphic representation of the deity which becomes relevant in iconic worship is here dispensed with ; it is the *mantra* that symbolises the deity when involved in a *yantra*. However, most of the ritual sequences in iconic worship (welcoming, seating, honouring, offering ceremonial bath, presenting fresh garments and decorations, offering food, waving fragrant lights, and so on) are also employed here. The most important sequence in both iconic worship and *yantra*-worship is infusing vitality (*prāṇa-pratishṭhā*) without which the icon is a mere doll and the *yantra* a mere geometrical desi n. This s.quence is an elaborate ritual, and is followed by oblations in fire (*homa*) and reflective repitition of the *mantra* a large number of times (*japa*). This detail is the distinguishing feature of the deity-specific *yantras*; the other two varieties do not necessarily involve it.

The divinities that generally receive worship are of seven types: (1) sectarian gods (Śiva, Vishṇu, Devī, Sūrya, Gaṇapati, etc.); (2) tutellary deities (*kula devatās*) which are honoured and worshipped in families for generations; (3) chosen deities (*ishṭa-devatās*), selected by the individual devotee in accordance with his ta te, temperament and inclination, or given by a preceptor; (4) household deities (*gṛha-devatās*), which are invoked for the safety of the members of the household and for eliminating the evil forces from the dwelling place; (5) the deities adored by the village or community as a whole (*grāma-devatās*) and receiving collective worship; (6) deities that govern the entire world (like the guardian-spirits of the directions or lokapālas, Prajāpati, the eleven Rudras, the twelve Ādityas etc.); and (7) the deity that is indwelling in ones own heart (*ātma-devatā*). Not all of them, however, are represented in *yantras* or have *mantras* which are specific. Nor are these exclusive groups. A chosen deity may also be the tutellary deity; a tutellary deity may also be the community-deity; it may also be the household deity.

The deities invoked in *yantras* are generally of the sectarian, chosen, tutellary or community types. The last type of deities, however, are represented in *yantras* that are magical in nature: Hanumān, Chaṇḍī, Durgā, Śāstā, Kālī, Bhairava, Gaṇeśa, Yellamma, Kārtavīrya and so on. These deity-specific *yantras* may or may not entail ritual sequences. But they would generally involve appropriate mantra or seed-syllables. The sectarian deities are reckoned as five-fold, collectively known as 'pañcha-brahma' : Gaṇapathi (with the 6-lettered *mantra*), Sūrya (8-lettered *mantra*), Devī (15-lettered *mantra*), Śiva (5-lettered *mantra*), and Vishṇu (12 lettered *mantra*). Their seed-syllables are collectively given as *Aim Hrīm Śrīm Sraiṁ Srauh.*

The *yantras* with chosen deities are meant to help achieve all aspirations, mundane as well as spiritual ; the *yantras* with tutell-ary deities are employed for prosperity of the family, and for general welfare. Both types of *yantras* serve to eliminate obstacles on the path of spiritual progress. The attendant-spirits of these deities, which are also invoked during the worship ritual, fall into three types : enlighteners or guides (*guru* or *yoginī*), guardians or protectors (*rakshākara*), and accomplishers or obstacle-removers (*artha-sādhaka*). They are allotted appropriate enclosures (*āvaraṇas*) within the *yantra*, and are symbolically represented by their seed-syllables.

Well-known among the deity-specific *yantra* are those that re-present the "ten great mothers" (*daśa mahāvidyā*) : Kālī (represent-ing the evolutionary principle of primordial time ; with the seed-syllable *Krīm*), Tārā (power of spiritual ascent, *Aum*), Shoḍaśī (perfection and totality, *Aim Klīm Sauh*), Bhuvaneśvarī space-consciousness, dimensionality, *Hrīm*), Chhinna mastā (ever devo-uring resurrection, *Hūm*), Bhairavī (power of destruction, *Hsraim Hsklrīm, Hsrauh*), Dhūmāvatī (death, despair, destruction, *Dhūm*), Bagalā-mukhī (unconscious tendencies leading to illusions, *Hlrīm*), Mātaṅgī (dominating over evil, *Aim, Hrīm Śrīm Aim Klīm Sauh*) and Kamalā (prosperity and purity, *Śrīm*). Each of them has a characteristic *yantra,* like the eight-petalled lotus within a circle for Kālī, star hexagon for Bhuvaneśvarī, hexagon within a eight-petalled lotus for Dhūmāvatī, hexagon within a circle for Kamalā. But all the ten are accommodated in the ten directions : Kālī in North, Shoḍaśī in North-East, Chhinnamastā in East, Dhūmāvatī in South East, Bagalā in South, Kamalā in South-West, Bhuvaneśvarī in West, Mātaṅgī in North-West, Tārā above and Bhairavi below.

Of these, three are most popularly worshipped : Kālī (in Eastern parts of the country and Nepal), Tārā (in Nepal, Tibet, Mongolia and China), and Shoḍaśī (all over the country in many forms such as Tripurā-sundarī, Rājarājeśvari, Bālā etc.). There are many medieval texts which describe the worship of these three divinities. There are numerous variant forms of these three which receive worship in the *yantra* form : Mahishamardinī, Durgā, Chāmuṇḍā, Śūlinī, Annapūrṇā, Pratyaṅgirā and so on. It may be noticed that most of the deity-specific *yantras* represent mother-goddesses. The celebrated Śri-chakra and its variant Bālā-*yantra* belong to this group. Yantras to Śiva are few ; but the attendant-spirits of Śiva have their own *yantras* (Bhairava, Vīrabhadra, Gaṇeśa, Bhūta-ḍāmara etc.). The Vishṇu-*yantras* represent mostly the *avatāra* aspects : Kṛishṇa, Rāma, Narasiṁha and Vāsudeva. Among the other male divinities that are worshipped in *yantras*, most of them are human heroes deified, like Kārtavīrya, Śāstā, Vaṭuka-bhairava and Mailāra.

The third major variety of *yantras* are essentially devices for concentrating the mind, focussing attention and channelising consciousness. They are generally referred to as 'maṇḍalas', especially in Tibet, China and Japan. Rightly are they described as psychocosmograms : they are models of the subjective space of the practitioner, incorporating the material and transactional world in which he is involved. Indian thought recognizes three space-orders : the three-dimensional space-bound world of normal experience (*mahākāśa*, meaning the presentational space) ; the subjective space of consciousness and its modalities (*chittākāśa*), and the space of pure consciousness which is fundamental to both the above spaces (*chidākāśa*). The maṇḍala is the map comprehending all three. It is employed in order to move from one order to the other : from world-space to subjective space, from subjective space to the being-space (undifferentiated, dimensionless consciousness). The actual layout of the maṇḍala involves this movement, the world-space being represented by the boundary-lines (the so-called *bhūpura*), the subjective space by the enclosures within, and the being-space by the central point (*bindu*).

It is the central point that is the most significant aspect of the maṇḍala : for the whole plan emanates from it, and finally gets dissolved in it. Each individual has his own central point, and his subjective space has its own central point, and the transactional world in which he finds himself has its own central point. It is because the three do not coincide that there is stress in life. Maṇḍala is a technique by which proper centering could be achieved Meditation is an attempt to harmonize ones psychic energies, and the layout of the mandala provides a model for this.

Self-actualization through a maṇḍala involves that the practitioner leaves the world of things and thoughts (which by its nature is fragmented, made diffuse, differentiated) and moves towards his own inner being which is beyond things and thoughts (which is unitary, wholesome and tranquil). In this movement, the maṇḍala layout provides him with the opportunity to reconcile the contraries, to visualize the inner dynamics, and to activate the psychic energies.

It is usual to employ *mantras* and *mudrās* while meditating on the maṇḍala The maṇḍala as the yantra represents the field of consciousness (*chitta*) ; mantra as the vocalized formula for repitition represents the expressive faculty of consciousness (vāk), and mudrā as physical posture and gesture represents the material vehicle in which the consciousness is embodied and through which it works (*kāya*). When a deity is also empoyed to preside over the maṇḍala, it is as a unifyi g agent.

IV

Rituals connected with the Yantra

The yantra is essentially a graphic design, and is therefore almost invariably inscribed on a flat surface. It is either drawn on palm leaf, bhūrja leaf or paper, or etched on a metal sheet or stone slab. Among metals, gold, silver and copper are mentioned as suitable, in the same order. Inscribed on a gold sheet, the yantra is effective for life, while inscribed on silver it is effective for twenty years, and on copper for six years. The yantra in gold is said to eliminate all obstacles, in silver it is said to make for general welfare, and in copper it ensures individual success While inscribing a yantra on metal, the pointed golden rod (*hema-śalākā*) is prescribed to be used as a pen.

The yantra drawn on a bhūrja leaf (birch bark) is said to be effective for twelve years, and the one on palm leaf for six years. The texts do not mention the yantras on paper, although their use has been extensive since medieval times. The dye used for drawing is prescribed to be a mixture of *kuṁkuma* (saffron, Crocus Sativus), *rochanā* (bright yellow pigment), *rakta-chandana* (red sandal, Caesalpina Sappan) and *jaṭāmāṅsī* (Nardostachys), in equal proportions. Red dye (*lākshā*) and musc (*kastūrī*) are also used. When the yantra is drawn or inscribed, it must be covered with yellow cloth and tied with silken threads until its consecration. No consecration is necessary when the yantra is meant to be worn on the body. Children wear the yantra of this type round their neck ; women wear it tied round their left arm, and men round their right arm.

Consecration of the yantra is especially indicated for the deity-specific variety. And so the consecration rituals are very similar to those that pertain to the consecration of icons. When the yantra has been drawn or inscribed by one who is pure in heart, chaste in conduct, pious in disposition, tranquil by temperament and well-versed in Āgama, then there would already be some power infused into the yantra, and the consecration would greatly be facilitated. Some preliminary rites of *yantra-saṁskāra* could be overlooked, like keeping the yantra immersed in the "bovine pentad" (*pañchagavya*), and cleansing it with the repitition of Om.

The normal procedure is to prepare the yantra preliminarily by em-powering it (*abhimantraṇa*) by repeating over it the mystic syllable *Haum* one hundred and eight times, before giving it a bath in *pañchagavya,* followed by a bath in milk, curds, ghee, honey, and sugar, ending with a bath in clean water. The yantra is then dried, and touched ceremonially by the blades of kuśa-grass while the *gāyatrī* hymn is being recited. The *gāyatrī* appropriate for this ritual assumes this form :

Yantra-rājāya vidmahe ; mahāyantrāya dhīmahi ;

tanno yantrah prachodayāt.

This is followed by the most important sequence of invoking life-force into the yantra (*prāṇa-pratishṭhā*). The yantra now becomes for all purposes a divinity and becomes fit for worship. Worship is conducted with five "services" (*upachāras*) as part of the consecration ritual. Then the yantra is covered by silken cloth and tied up with silken thread ; and the mantra appropriate for the yantra is recited one thousand times, before 'offerings' (*bali*) are made to it. Finally, some oblations in fire (*homa*) are also offered ; and gifts are given to the needy. Details of consecration are given in several texts like *Vāmakeśvara-tantra*.

The yantra becomes unfit for use if it breaks, cracks up, gets burnt, or falls on the ground ; its power gets lost if it is touched by unclean persons, wicked folk, or when worshipped by a mantra not appropriate to it. If the yantra is damaged, stolen or touched by fire, the devotee is required to fast for a day and repeat the *mantra* one lakh times. The damaged or burnt yantra is to be dropped in a river or in sea.

The drawing of the yantra is to be done by free hand, and not by the use of instruments. And the entire yantra with all its enclosures and figures must be completed in one sitting, and with single-minded attention. While drawing the yantra, the writer must be engaged in continually repeating the chosen mantra. Each enclosure or figure must be drawn at one stretch, viz. without lifting the pen or stylus from the palm leaf or metal sheet.

There are two methods in drawing : one begins with the central point and gradually moves towards the outermost figure, and the other beginning with the outermost figure moves towards the central point. The former is described as the method of successive emanation or spread (*vistāra*) ; and the latter is the method of of successive withdrawal or absorption (*saṅkocha*). Alternatively, they are known as the methods of creation (*sṛshṭi*) and destruction (*saṁhāra*) ; ercation is movement away from the central point while destruction (actually absorption or assimilation) is a movement towards the central point. The yantras that facilitate meditation (leading to concentration and tranquility) are usually drawn following the method of absorption, while all other yantras are drawn following the other method.

After the drawing, the most important step is the accommodation os the seed-syllables and the mantra within the layout of the yantra. Along with these details, the entire alphabet of Sanskrit speech (representing the bridge between the world of things and the world of thoughts) is also included in the yantra. If the space or arrangement of enclosures does not allow all the fifty letters of the alphabet to be written, then the mnemonic formula (*saṅkocha-mantra*) is preferred : "Om AKaChaṬaTaPaYaŚaHaLom". This formula is made up of the initial letters of the vowel group and the consonant groups, sandwiched between the *praṇavas* : 'A' symbolizes all the sixten vowels ; the following five letters represent the five consonant-groups and the last four letters represent "air", "fire", "water" and "earth". Thus the four elements which are the bricks of the entire material world, and the fifth element (*ākāśa*) from which the entire psychological universe emanates are comprehended in this formula.

Vātula-tantra discusses the mystic import of the letters of the alphabet as they are included within the yantra. The letters are grouped into 'masculine', 'feminine' and 'neuter'. Among vowels, 'a', 'i', 'u', 'e', o', and 'aṁ' are 'masculine'. 'ā', 'ī', 'ū', 'āi', 'au', and 'ah' are 'feminine'., and 'ṛi', 'ṛī', 'lṛi', and 'lṛī' are 'neuter'. Among the consonants, 'ka', 'ga', 'cha', 'ja', 'ṭa', 'ḍa', 'ta', 'da', 'pa', 'ba', 'sha', and 'ṇa' are 'masculine' ; 'kha', 'gha', 'chha', 'jha', 'ḍha', 'tha', dha', 'pha', 'bha', da', and 'sa' are 'feminine,, and 'ṅa', 'ña', 'ṇa'. 'na', 'ma', 'ya', 'ra', 'la', 'va', and 'ḷa' are 'neuter'. There are six vowels and twelve consonants in each of the two groups ('masculine' and 'feminine'), totalling eighteen in each group. There are four vowels and ten consonants in the 'neuter' group, totalling fourteen. Excluding the 'neuter' group, there are twelve vowels and twenty-four consonants, totalling thirty-six. Now these numbers (4, 6, 10, 12, 16, 18, 24 and 36) suggest the geometrical designs that possibly constitute a yantra. A yantra, in principle, is the representation of the 'masculine' (Śiva) and 'feminine' (Śakti) principles of phenomenal existence. The different modes of the interaction between these two principles explain the differences that obtain between various yantras. The letters of the alphabet, especially the vowels (which can occur without the involvement of consonants), are called the "aspects" (*kalā*) of the mother-goddess.

The same Tantra also explains the correspondance between the basic elements and the vowels of the alphabet The first three vowels ('a', 'ā' and 'i') are the *ākāśa* element ; the next three ('ī' 'u' and 'ū') the air element ; the following three ('ṛi', 'ṛī' and 'lṛī') the fire element ; the next three ('e', 'ai' and 'o') the water element ; and the last three ('au', 'aṁ' and 'ah') the earth element. Even as the elements from *ākāśa* to earth are increasingly material, so the vowels from 'a' to 'ah' are increasingly expressive The vewel 'a' is all the divinities in an undifferentiated state. The second vowel 'ā' is the great power (*parāśakti*) to project and generate ; 'i' is Vishṇu, the principle of universal pervasion ; 'ī' is *māyā*, the principle of creation ; 'u' is *vāstu* or material foundation ; 'ū' is *bhū* or earth-ground ; 'ṛi' is the first progenitor or Brahmā-Prajāpati ; 'ṛī' is the principle of variegation (śikhaṇḍin) 'lṛi' are the twin planners of celestial well-being (the Āśvins) ; 'e' is Vīrabhadra or the priniciple of overcoming obstacles ; 'ai' is Sarasvatī or the principle of expression by speech ; 'o' is Īśvara or the lord of phenomena ; 'au' is the primordial power to accomlish all objectives, Ādi-śakti ; 'aṁ' is the masculine consort of this power, Bhairava ; and 'ah' is the deity conjointly produced by power and pleasure (Kālarudra)

There is another way of classifying the letters of the alphabet. The vowels (16) are described as "active" (*rājasa*), the five groups of consonants (25) as "sluggish or dark" (*tāmasa*), and the consonants 'śa', 'sha', 'sa', 'va', 'la', 'ra', 'ya', and 'ma' (8), as "good and bright" (*sāttvika*). The yantra prescribed in *Vātula-tantra* accommodates the letters of the alphabet in this order : the first enclosure outside the focal area is the eight-petalled lotus, in the petals of which the eight "sāttvika" letters are inscribed ; the next enclosure is the sixteen-petalled lotus in which the "rājasa" letters are inscribed ; and the third enclosre is the lotus with twenty-five petals, in each of which a 'tāmasa" letter is inscribed. The "sāttvika" letters are nearest to the focal area, in which a four-petalled lotus is placed, each petal representing a seed-syllable : 'sa' to the East, 'a' to the South, 'ai' to the West and 'ksha" to the North. These four symbolize Śakti (power to preserve), Śiva (the ultimate good, or emancipation), Ātman (the Self, which is the storehouse of all accomplishment), and Vidyā (wisdom, which is bliss) respectively ; and they are alternately described as Sthiti, Mukti, Siddhi and Sukha. The central point of the yantra has 'ha', which is the seed-syllable of Śiva, whose yantra it is.

In many yantras, however, the accommodation of the letters of the alphabet is implied and not inscribed. They may, on the other hand, contain mantras in various dispositions. Rituals pertaining to such yantras take the form of "puraścharaṇa" ("moving towards the deity with the appropriate mantra as the guide"). The purpose is to 'accomplish' the mantra of the deity of ones own choice (*sveshṭa-devatā-mantra-siddhi*). It assumes a five-fold sequence ; *japa* (repitition of the mantra as prescribed), fire-oblations (*homa*), water-oblations (*tarpaṇa*), bath-offering (*abhisheka*), and feeding the needy and the deserving (*bhojana*) (*Yoginī-hṛdaya*). There are several texts (like *Puraścharaṇa-chandrika*, *Rahasya-puraścharaṇa-vidhi*, etc,) which give details of the time, place, manner, restrictions, regulations, and permissible deviations with regard to this procedure which is also called the 'five-fold worship' (*pañchāṅgopāsanā*.)

Each mantra is said to have the following aspects : the sage who is the author of the mantra (*ṛshi*), the meter in which the mantra is composed (*chhandas*), the deity for whom the mantra is meant (*devatā*), the seed of the mantra (*bīja*), the power of the mantra (*śakti*), the 'peg' to which the mantra is tied, viz. the activating principle (*kīlaka*), and the purpose for which the mantra is employed (*viniyoga*). If the mantra is regarded as having a human form, the sage is its head, the meter its mouth (or face), the deity its heart, the seed its navel, the power its private organ and the 'peg' its feet The deity who is invoked by the mantra assumes the form of the mantra, and the mantra assumes the form of the universe :

"mantras tu devatā-rūpam mantra-rūpam idam jagat"

(*Vātulāgama*)

And the universe is represented by the yantra. Thus there is an equivalence between the deity and the mantra, the mantra and the yantra.

The mantra (whatever the aspects mentioned above) has five "shoots" (*pañcha-pallava*). A shoot (or sprout) in this context signifies the emergent attitude with which the mantra terminates. The body of the mantra contains the seed-syllables and the name of the deity ; the devotee's disposition towards, or orientation with regard to, the deity should find articulation at the end of the mantra, and this is the 'pallava'. Without this feature, the mantra is described as 'naked' ("pallavena vinā mantro nagnas tu parikīrtitah"). The deity is then not properly represented in the sense that the devotee has not specified how he stands with regard to the deity. The five 'shoots' which the mantras may possibly have are : 'namah', 'svāhā', 'vaushaṭ', 'hūm', 'phaṭ'. Each of them has its own special significance and situational relevance. 'Namah" means prostration ; 'svāhā' signifies offering ; 'vaushaṭ' is will to be protected ; 'hūm' is the call to drive away (evil forces) and "phaṭ' is the urge to break (the obstacles) down.

The mantra is invariably preceded by the articulation (or rather ejaculation) : 'om', which has the significance of submission, acceptance (of the deity) and inviting the attention of the deity. It is said that the expression 'om' is like unto the head of the deity, while the 'shoot' (pallava) is the deity's feet. The expression 'om' is followed by the seed-syllable specific to the diety, which in turn may be followed by the chosen name of the deity. Thus, 'om' and the *pallava* are common to all the mantras ; the mantras differ only with regard to the particular form of the divinity visualized. The central point in a yantra is usually taken as the position of the expresssion 'om'. and the outermost figure (square or circle) as the *pallava*. In between these two limits, the deity is projected in terms of the body of the yantra.

Along with the repitition of the specific mantra, worship

rituals also include often (but not necessarily) the reading of supplementary texts like the appropriate hymnology (*gītā*), the cluster of names (*nāmāvalī*), adulations and prayers (*stava*), armour or protective devices (*kavacha*), and the heart-formulae (*hṛdaya*), all specific to the deity who is represented in the yantra.

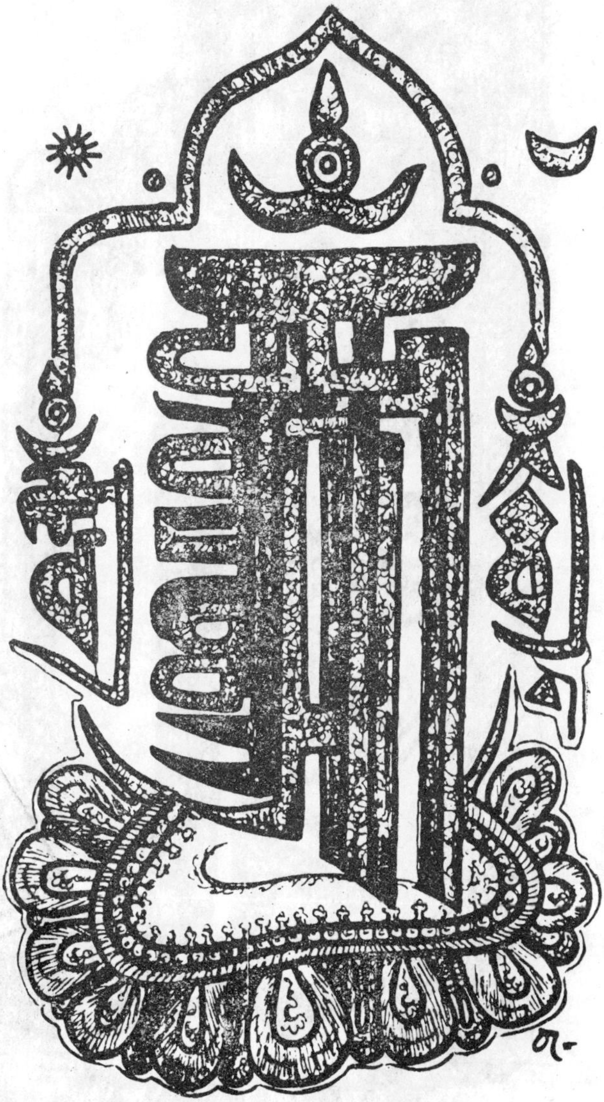

Fig. 1. Composite letter yantra from Tibet,

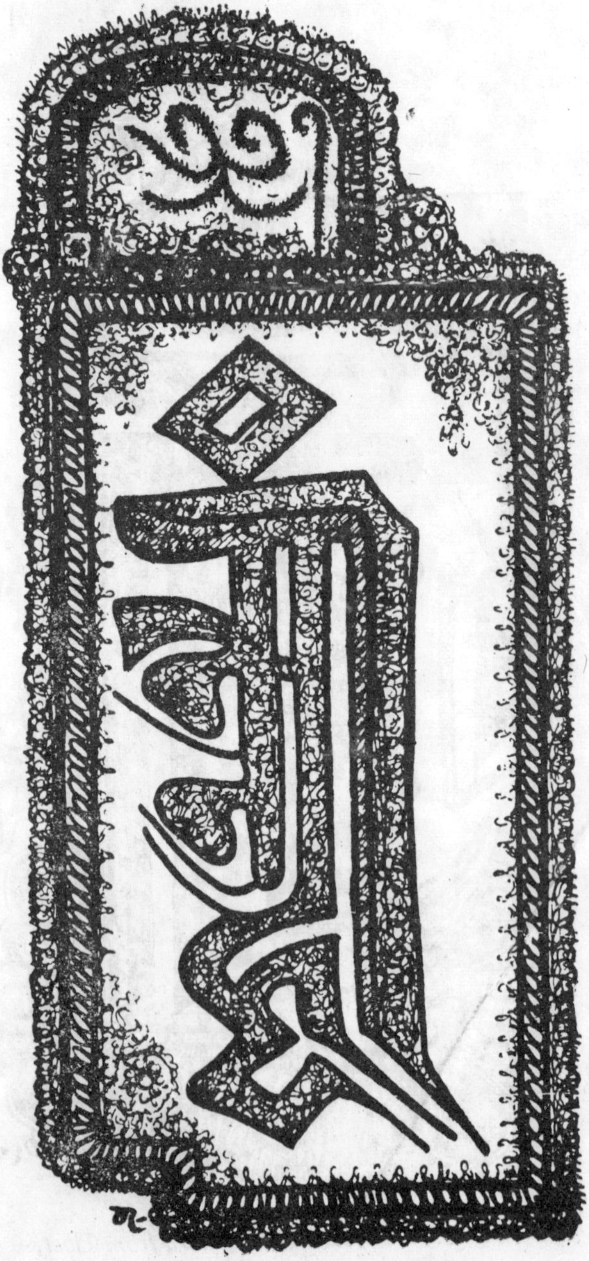

Fig. 2. Another letter-yantra from Tibet.

Fig. 3. *Another letter-yantra from Tibet; verbal symbols in the from of a deity worship.*

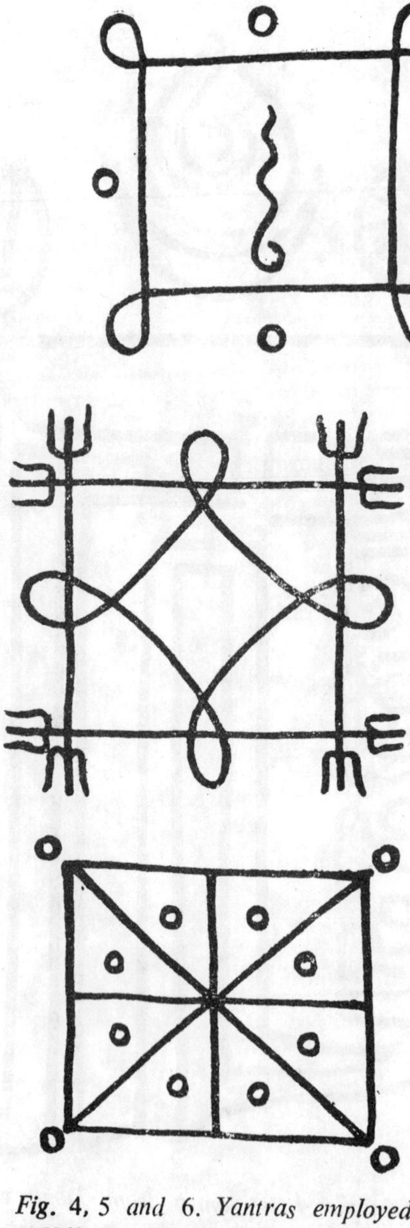

Fig. 4, 5 *and* 6. *Yantras employed in Villages of South India for protection of cattle.*

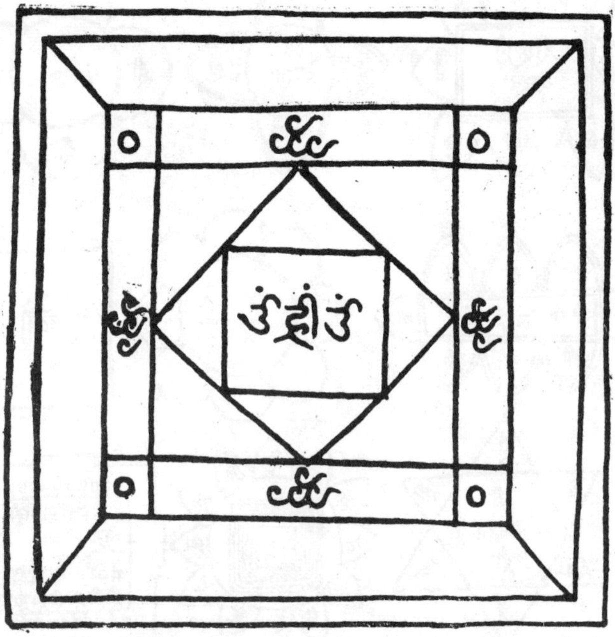

Fig. 7. *An illustration of the yantra containing forms representing energies in various modes.*

Fig 8. *Illustration of the employment of sheveral geometrical forms in the yantra*

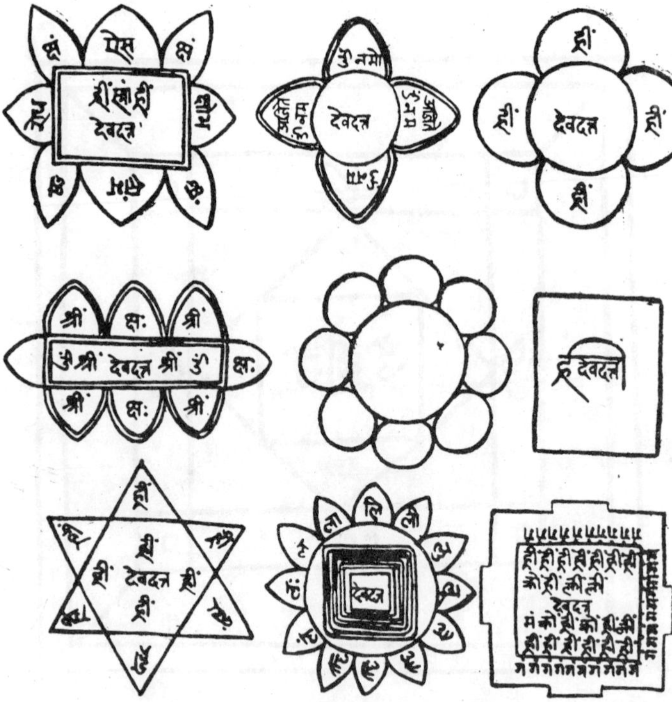

Fig. 9. *Yantras for personal safety, health and prosperity*

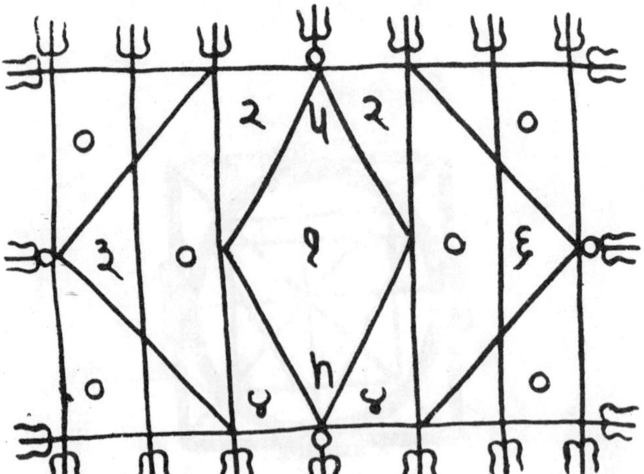

Fig. 10. *A Protective yantra*

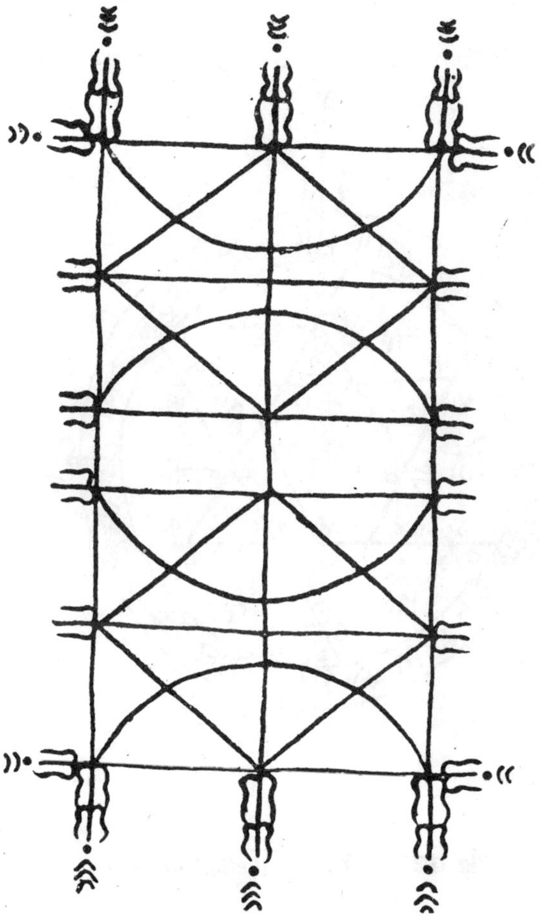

Fig. 11. *Another protective yantra*

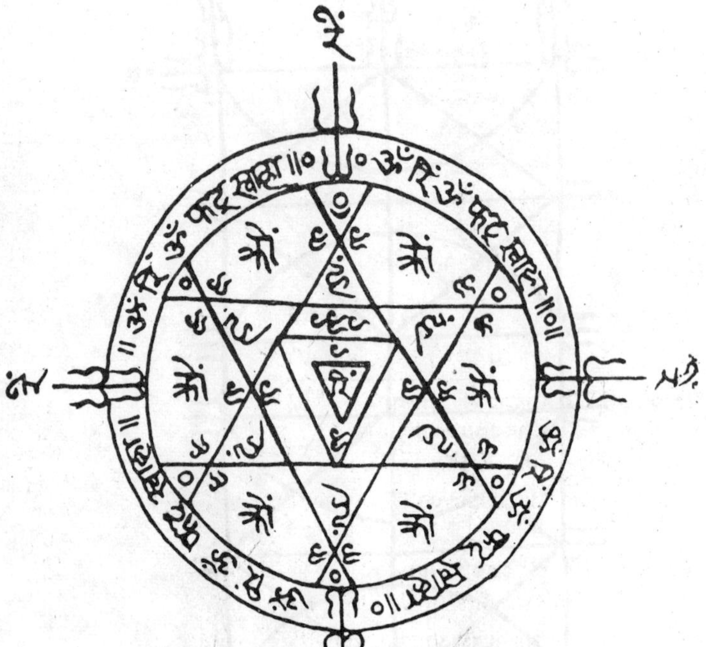

Fig. 12. *A Yantra to eliminate evil*

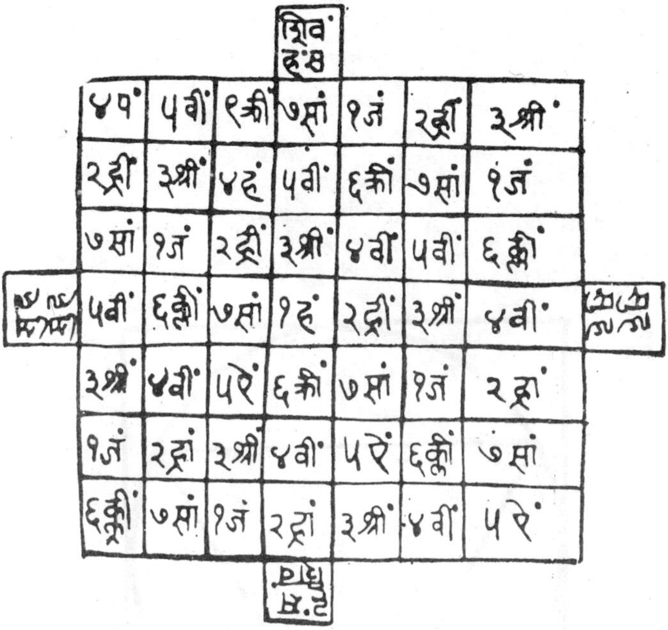

Fig 13, *A yantra combining mystic numerals and letters for magical purposes*

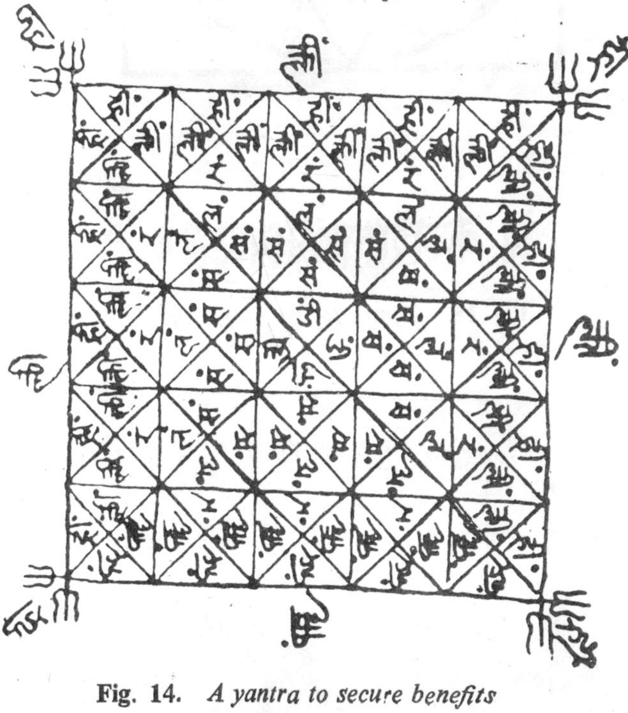

Fig. 14. *A yantra to secure benefits*

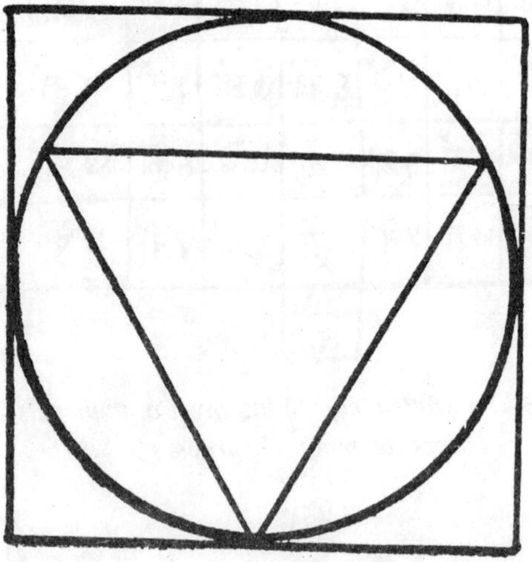

॥ कलशस्थापनामण्डल ॥

Fig. 15. *Yantra for consecration*

Fig. 16. *Another yantra for consecration*

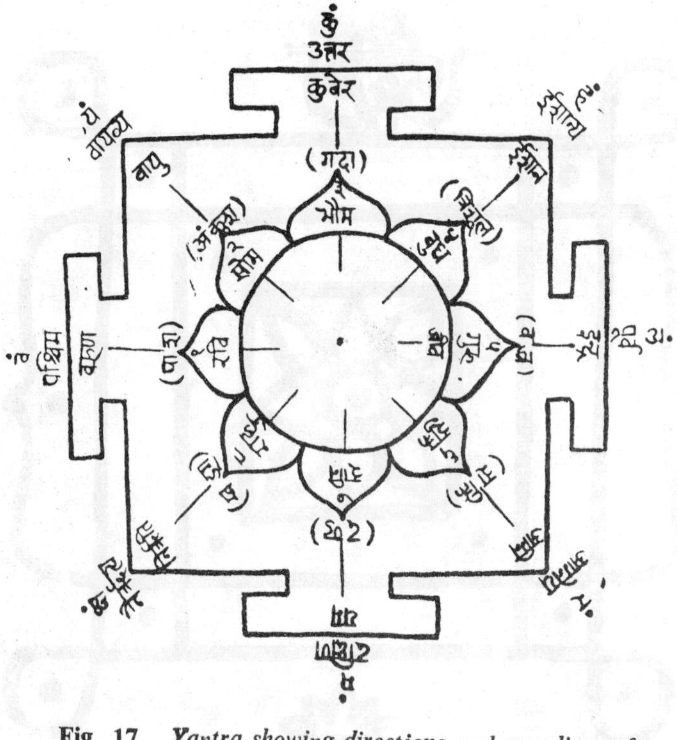

Fig. 17. *Yantra showing directions and guardians of directions*

(द्रां द्राविण्यै । क्षों क्षोभिण्यै । बं बन्धिन्यै । मों मोहिन्यै । आं आकर्षिण्यै । नमः ॥)

(यन्त्रान्तरम्) त्रिकोणमादौ आय पञ्चकोणं अष्टाब्जयुग्मेन्दुकसंकुलानि ।
वस्वब्जवेदास्त्रयुत भूपुराणि मातङ्गकन्या नयेन्नमादुः ॥
(सुरेन्द्रसंहितोक्तं)

॥ राजमातङ्गीयन्त्रम् ॥

Fig. 18. *The yantra of Rāja-mātangi for magical benefits*

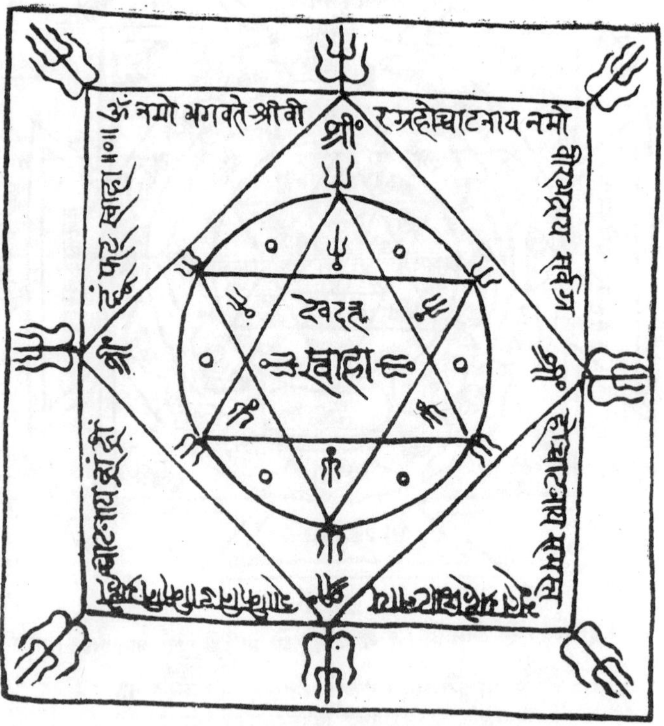

Fig. 19. *Yantra for removal of evil influences*

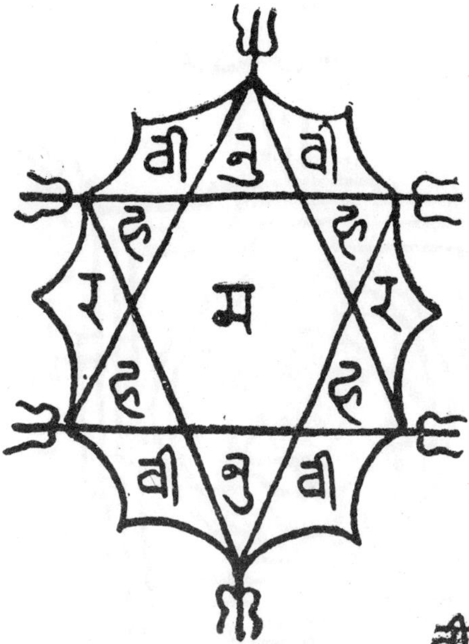

वीरहनुमयन्त्र

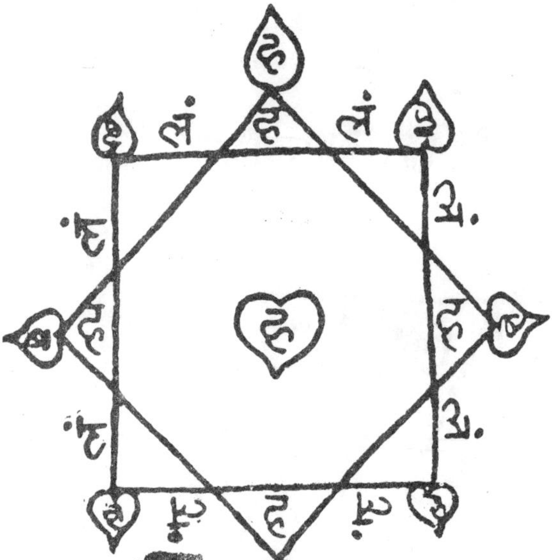

रामदूतयन्त्र

Fig. 20, 21. *Yantras of Hanuman for protection*

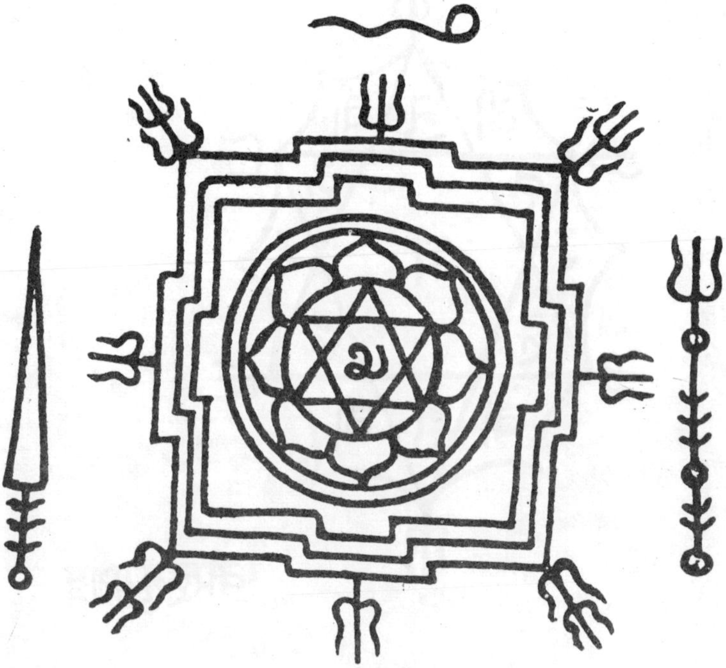

Fig. 22 *Yantra of Khaḍga-rāvaṇa for welfare of children*

॥ खड्गरावणबलि ॥

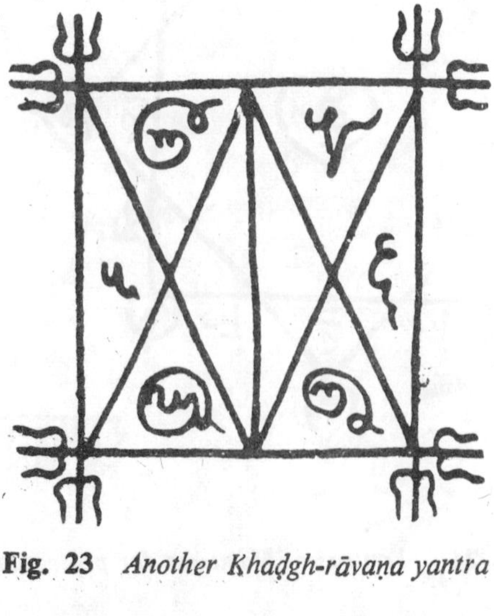

Fig. 23 *Another Khaḍgh-rāvaṇa yantra*

चतुर्भिः शिवचक्रैश्च शक्तिचक्रैश्च पञ्चभिः ।
नवचक्रैश्च संसिद्धं श्रीचक्रं शिवयोर्वपुः ॥

Fig. 24 *Śrī-yantra of the Mother- goddess*

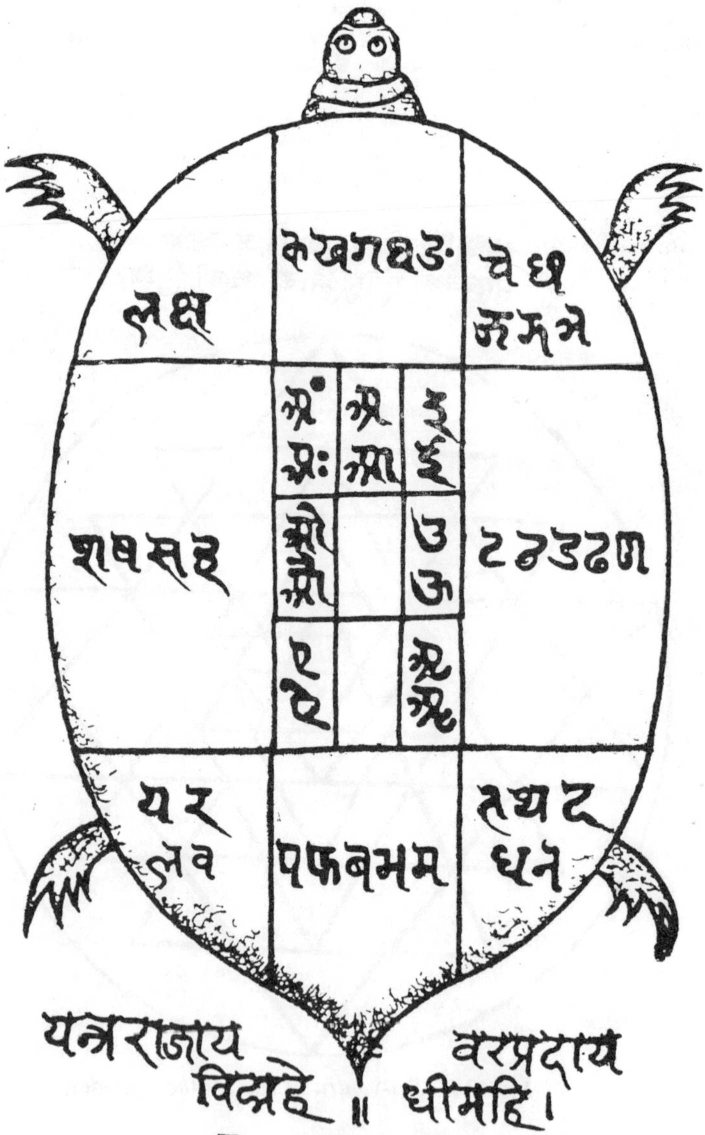

Fig. 25. *Kūrma-yantra for extraction of mantra*

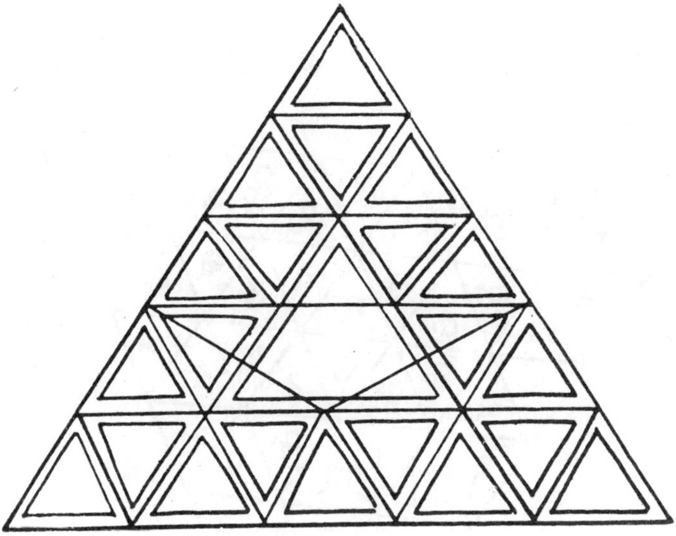

॥ यन्त्रोद्धारयन्त्र ॥

Fig. 26, *A yantra for extraction of yantras*

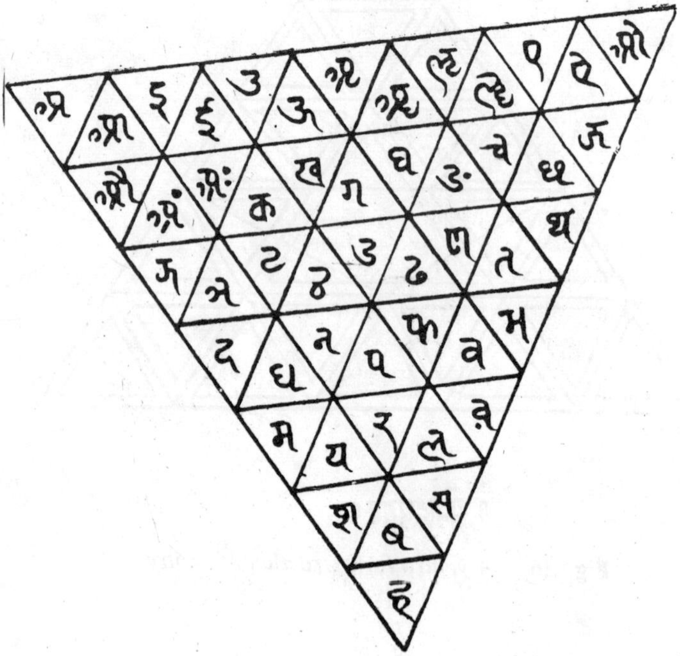

Fig. 27. *Yantra for extraction of mantra*

Fig. 28. *Another yantra for the same purpose*

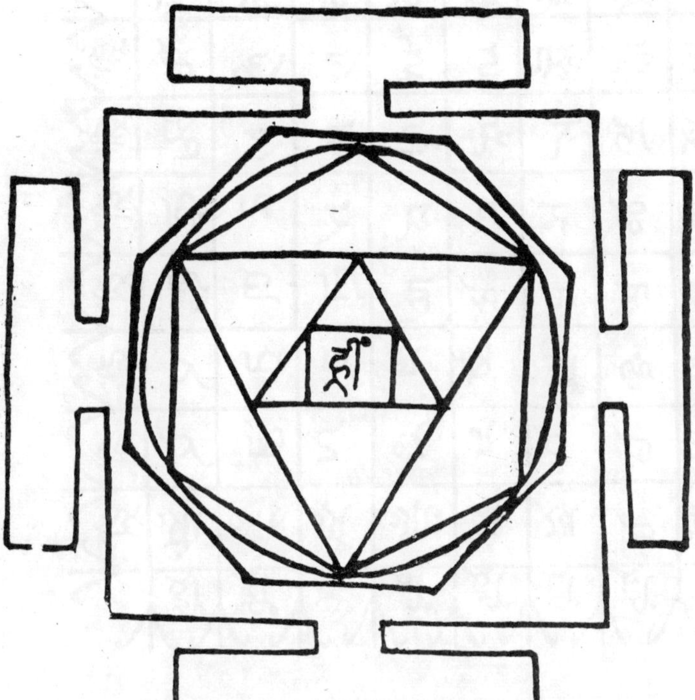

Fig. 29 *A composite yantra*

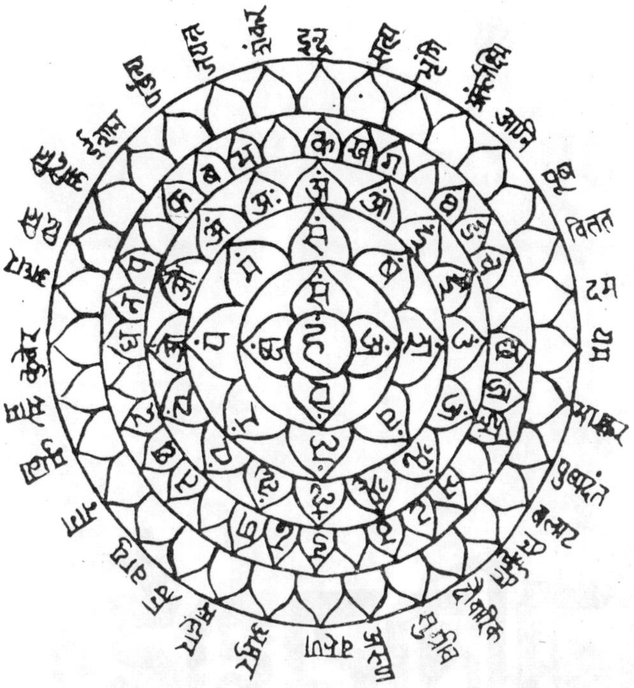

Fig, 30 *Yantra with letters inscribed*

१४	१७	२	१२	१५	६	४	३	५	८	९
आ	इ	उ	ऋ	ऌ	ए	ऐ	ओ	औ	अं	अः
क	ख	ग	घ	ङ	च	छ	ज	झ	ञ	ट
ठ	ड	ढ	ण	त	थ	द	ध	न	प	फ
ब	भ	म	य	र	ल	व	श	ष	स	ह
१०	१	७	४	८	३	७	५	४	१	७

Fig. 31. *A chart of letters and numcrols for preparation of yantras*

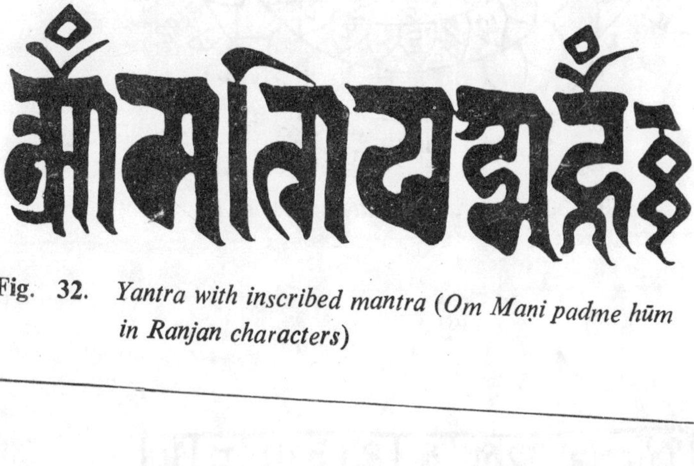

Fig. 32. *Yantra with inscribed mantra (Om Maṇi padme hūm in Ranjan characters)*